One Well

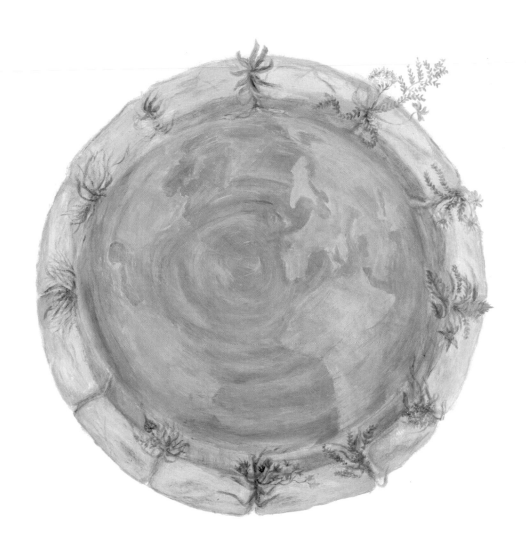

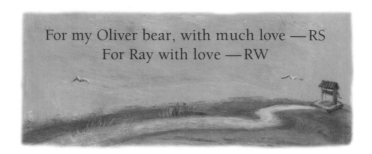

For my Oliver bear, with much love — RS
For Ray with love — RW

ACKNOWLEDGMENTS

I am truly grateful to the many individuals who have made this book possible. My deepest gratitude goes to Valerie Wyatt for her wonderful insights and unfailing guidance and support. Many thanks also to Marie Bartholomew for creating such an inspiring vision and Rosemary Woods for bringing the book to life. Special thanks to Valerie Hussey for patiently allowing me to wade through the content until I found the story. I also want to thank Melissa Clark, Rosanne Metz and my family for eagerly reading drafts and listening to all my watery tales.

Once again, I must praise my incredible team of technical and educational reviewers: Joanne DiCosimo, Mark Graham and Paul Hamilton at the Canadian Museum of Nature; Charles Hopkins, UNESCO Chair and UN University Chair, York University in Toronto, Canada; and Susan Gesner of Gesner and Associates Environmental Learning. Thank you for sharing your wisdom.

I am also grateful to the Ontario Arts Council for their financial support.

Finally, two major events occurred while I was writing this book. The Asian tsunami and Hurricane Katrina will forever be reminders of the power of water. My thoughts continue to be with those whose lives have been affected by these disasters.

CitizenKid™ is a trademark of Kids Can Press Ltd.

Kids Can Press acknowledges the financial support of the Government of Ontario, through the Ontario Media Development Corporation's Ontario Book Initiative; the Ontario Arts Council; the Canada Council for the Arts; and the Government of Canada, through the CBF, for our publishing activity.

Published in Canada by
Kids Can Press Ltd.
25 Dockside Drive
Toronto, ON M5A 0B5

Published in the U.S. by
Kids Can Press Ltd.
2250 Military Road
Tonawanda, NY 14150

www.kidscanpress.com

Edited by Val Wyatt
Designed by Marie Bartholomew

This book is smyth sewn casebound.

Manufactured in Malaysia in 9/2014
by Tien Wah Press (Pte) Ltd.

CM 07 20 19 18 17 16 15 14

Library and Archives Canada Cataloguing in Publication

Strauss, Rochelle, 1967–
   One well : the story of water on Earth / written by Rochelle Strauss ; illustrated by Rosemary Woods.

For ages 8 and up.
ISBN 978-1-55337-954-6

1. Water — Juvenile literature. I. Woods, Rosemary II. Title.

QH90.16.S87 2007   j553.7   C2006-903701-9

FSC
www.fsc.org
MIX
Paper from responsible sources
FSC® C012700

Kids Can Press is a CORUS™ Entertainment company

One Well
The Story of Water on Earth

WRITTEN BY Rochelle Strauss

ILLUSTRATED BY Rosemary Woods

CitizenKid™

A collection of books that inform children about the
world and inspire them to be better global citizens

Kids Can Press

One Well

Imagine for a moment that all the water on Earth came from just one well.

This isn't as strange as it sounds. All water on Earth *is* connected, so there really *is* just one source of water — one global well — from which we all draw our water. Every ocean wave, every lake, stream and underground river, every raindrop and snowflake and every bit of ice in glaciers and polar icecaps is part of this global well.

So whether you are turning on a faucet in North America, pulling water from a well in Kenya or bathing in a river in India, it is all the same water. And because it is all connected, how we treat the water in the well will affect every species on the planet, including us, now and for years to come.

Earth is the only planet that has liquid water and is therefore the only planet that can support life.

You need water, and so does every other living organism — every person, every plant and every animal. Without water, nothing can survive.

The amount of water on Earth hasn't ever changed. It has been the same for billions of years.

5

The Water in the Well

We live on a watery planet. Almost 70 percent of Earth's surface is covered with water. This surface water is found in oceans, lakes, rivers, streams, marshes, even in puddles and the morning dew. There is so much water that if you looked down at Earth from space, it would appear blue.

But there is also water we can't see, beneath the Earth's surface. This "groundwater" can be found just about everywhere — it fills the cracks in rocks and the spaces between rocks, grains of sand and soil. Most groundwater is close to the Earth's surface, but some of it is buried quite deep. Water is also frozen in glaciers and polar icecaps. And there is water in the atmosphere.

Every one of these water sources feeds Earth's One Well.

WHERE IS THE WATER ON EARTH?

Oceans	97.23 percent
Icecaps and glaciers	2.14 percent
Groundwater	0.61 percent
Freshwater lakes	0.009 percent
Inland saltwater seas	0.008 percent
Moisture in the soil	0.005 percent
Water in the atmosphere	0.001 percent
Rivers	0.0001 percent

Yes, there is more water in the atmosphere and soil than in all of Earth's rivers.

Recycling Water in the Well

The water you drank today may have rained down on the Amazon rainforest five years ago. A hundred years ago, it may have been steam escaping a teapot in India. Ten thousand years ago, it may have flowed in an underground river. A hundred thousand years ago, it may have been frozen solid in a glacier. And a hundred million years ago, it may have quenched the thirst of a dinosaur.

The amount of water on Earth doesn't change — there's no more water now than when the dinosaurs walked the Earth. The same water just keeps going through a cycle over and over again. This constant movement of water is called the water cycle.

During the water cycle, water evaporates from oceans, lakes, rivers, ponds and puddles, even from plants and animals. It rises into the air as water vapor.

As water vapor rises, it cools into tiny water droplets. This is called condensation. These droplets form clouds. Gradually, clouds collect more and more water droplets. The average white cloud weighs about twice as much as a blue whale.

When water droplets get too heavy, they fall from the clouds in the form of hail, snow or rain. This precipitation returns to oceans, lakes and rivers. It also seeps into the soil and down into the groundwater. Year after year, water continuously circulates through the water cycle.

The Water Cycle

In one year, an area of rainforest the size of a football field pumps over 75 000 L (19 700 U.S. gal.) of water vapor into the atmosphere—more than enough to fill a backyard swimming pool.

It takes about one million tiny water droplets to make just one raindrop.

Why are the oceans salty? Rivers flow into the sea, collecting salt from rocks and soil and adding it to the ocean. As ocean water evaporates, the salt is left behind.

How thirsty is a tree? On a summer's day, an average-sized birch tree can draw about 300 L (80 U.S. gal.) of water from the soil. That's almost enough water to fill two large bathtubs.

Many plants depend on water to disperse their seeds. A coconut (the seed of a palm tree) can spend weeks, months or even years drifting in the ocean before reaching land and sprouting.

The plants you eat are mostly water. Tomatoes are about 95 percent water. Apples are about 85 percent water. Seeds are among the driest foods —they contain only 5 to 10 percent water.

Plants at the Well

The first plants on Earth began life in the water. About 450 million years ago, some were washed ashore. At first they could live only in wet areas. Gradually they developed root systems that allowed them to tap into water in the soil.

Water is essential to plants. In fact, plants are mostly water. It's the water in their cells that gives them their shape and form—without it, they droop and shrivel.

Water also helps plants make food for themselves. Plants use the sun's energy to change water and carbon dioxide into simple sugars that feed the plant. This process is called photosynthesis. Water then helps carry this food throughout the plant.

During photosynthesis, plants also release water vapor into the air. Roots absorb water, which is carried to the stem. The stem acts like a water pipe in your house, moving water through the plant to the leaves. From the leaves, water is released back into the atmosphere. This is called transpiration. The water that is transpired is added to the cycle of water on Earth.

Water is important to plants, but plants are also important to water. Plant roots anchor soil and stop it from blowing or washing into lakes and rivers. Leaves and branches trap rainwater, allowing it to seep slowly into the soil instead of flowing quickly away. And trees provide shade, which helps keep moisture in the soil.

Plants depend on water from the well for survival, and the well depends on plants to help move water through its cycle. Without plants, the water cycle would be disrupted. Without water, plants could not survive.

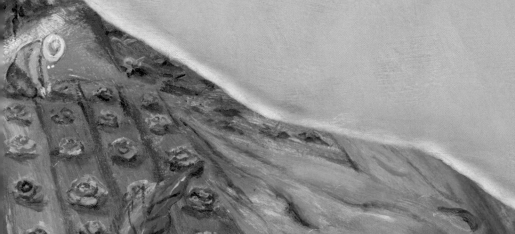

Animals at the Well

Like plants, animals (including you) are mostly made of water. The water in animals is very important. It carries nutrients, helps digestion, removes waste, controls temperature, cleans eyes and lubricates (oils) joints.

Water habitats are also home to many of Earth's animals, and are where many animals find their food. Watery species, such as fish, crabs, shrimp and zooplankton, are an important part of food chains around the world. A food chain is the link that connects animals (and other species), based on who eats whom. Without water-based species, food chains and food webs (collections of food chains) would collapse. Animals would starve.

Animals not only need water to survive, they are also part of the water cycle. Animals add water to the atmosphere by breathing, sweating, peeing and even drooling. The water you brushed your teeth with today may have been the spray of a beluga whale ten years ago.

Some of the "wettest" animals on Earth are the jellyfish. They are about 95 percent water. Frogs and earthworms are about 80 percent water, while dogs, elephants and humans are about 70 percent water.

All animals need water to drink, even desert animals. They get much of the water they need from the food they eat.

Animal life began in the ocean. Then, about 360 million years ago, some animals started to evolve. Their bodies began to change and they slowly adapted to living on land.

Saltwater marshes are wetlands that occur where the land meets the sea. These habitats are home to a wide diversity of species, from microscopic bacteria, fungi and algae to fish, crustaceans, reptiles, birds and mammals.

Some rainforest frogs, insects, spiders, worms and bacteria live their entire lives in the tiny pools of water that get trapped by the leaves of the bromeliad plant.

Watery Habitats

How can fish live in frozen lakes? Water freezes from the top down, but it rarely freezes right through. The ice at the surface is like a blanket that keeps the water below from freezing.

A habitat is a place where an animal can find everything it needs to live — food, shelter, space and water. Water is such an important part of an animal's habitat that if there isn't enough available, the animal will move away, even if all its other needs are met.

Most animals depend entirely on watery places, such as oceans, lakes and wetlands, for their habitat. Freshwater habitats (lakes, rivers, streams) are home to about 12 percent of all the animal species in the world. Saltwater habitats (oceans, seas and some saltwater lakes) are home to 60 percent of all fish species, as well as many other species, including some mammals and reptiles (such as whales, turtles and sea snakes).

Some of these animals live their whole lives in water and wouldn't survive out of it. Others, such as frogs, toads and many insects, spend part of their lives in the water and part on land. Whether water is their habitat or just part of their habitat, animals could not survive without it.

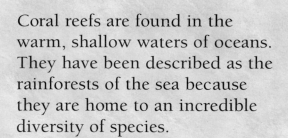

Coral reefs are found in the warm, shallow waters of oceans. They have been described as the rainforests of the sea because they are home to an incredible diversity of species.

People at the Well

Since the beginning of time, people have depended on water—for drinking, for food, for bathing and for watering their crops. Water has always provided a highway to move people and products from place to place. As cities and societies grow, so does their need for water.

Today, water is essential in our homes, in industry and in agriculture. At home we use water for cleaning, cooking, drinking, flushing toilets and for bathing. But homes account for only 10 percent of all the freshwater used.

About 21 percent of the water we use goes to make everything from computers to cars. Water is used in hydroelectric plants to generate electricity and in petroleum plants to make gas. In factories, water is used to heat things up or cool things down and to wash away waste. Water vapor (steam) even runs machinery. Water is also an ingredient in many products, such as lotions, shampoos, chemicals and drinks.

The remaining 69 percent of the freshwater we use goes into agriculture. Farms use huge amounts of water for crops and livestock.

Look around—almost everything you see was made using water. It took about 130 L (34 U.S. gal.) of water to make your bike. Water was used to grow and make the food you eat and the clothes you wear. Water was even used to make the paper for this book— and the ink used to print the words.

It takes about 185 L (49 U.S. gal.) of water to produce just one glass of milk. This includes the water the cow drinks, the water used to grow food for the cow and the water needed to process the milk.

About 147 000 L (38 800 U.S. gal.) of water was needed to make your family's car.

In North American homes, the bathroom is where about three-quarters of all water is used. One flush of the toilet uses nearly 13 L (3 ½ U.S. gal.).

A lot of water is required to produce the food you eat. Approximately 5200 L (1375 U.S. gal.) of water is needed just to make one fast food lunch (burger, fries and a soda).

Nearly a billion people around the world depend on fish as their primary source of protein.

Thirsty? People drink an average of 2 ½ L (⅔ U.S. gal.) of water a day. In your lifetime, you will drink the equivalent of a backyard swimming pool full of water.

Lake Baikal in southeast Siberia contains almost one-fifth of all the freshwater on Earth. It's also home to the Baikal seal, one of the world's few freshwater seals.

Approximately 0.001 percent of all water on Earth is in the atmosphere. If a tanker truck represents all the water on Earth, the water in the atmosphere would barely fill a third of a pop can.

The Bering Glacier in Alaska is the largest glacier in North America. It's about five times bigger than New York City and nearly twice as tall as the Empire State Building.

Around the world, more than half the drinking water we use comes from underground aquifers — layers of gravel, porous (holey) rocks or soil that trap large amounts of water.

Freshwater in the Well

Though we live on a watery planet, not all of that water can be used to meet our needs. That's because we humans and many other species depend on freshwater, and supplies of freshwater are limited.

Most of the water on Earth is saltwater — almost 97 percent. Only 3 percent is freshwater. If a tanker truck filled with water represented all the water on Earth, then the water used to fill a large bathtub would represent all of the planet's freshwater.

But most of the freshwater — over 99 percent — is frozen in icecaps and glaciers, trapped deep underground or in the atmosphere, so we can't use it. How much freshwater is available to us? Remember that bathtub? Imagine filling nine pop cans from it. This represents all the freshwater we can use.

While there is a lot of water on the planet, we have access to less than 1 percent of it.

Access to the Well

Some families are lucky. They can turn on the tap for drinking water, to fill a bathtub, wash their car or water the garden. But other families around the world are less fortunate. One billion people, almost 16 percent of Earth's population, have to walk more than fifteen minutes to get to the nearest water supply. There, they gather water for the day—just a few jugs, barely enough for drinking, cooking and cleaning. Other families don't have access to enough water to meet even these most basic needs.

While the amount of water on Earth is always the same, the *distribution* of water across the world isn't. Huge differences in rainfall can happen from country to country and even within the same country. Less rainfall means less water available in lakes, rivers and aquifers. Sometimes there just isn't enough water where it's needed most.

Because water is not evenly distributed across the globe, nearly one-fifth of the world's population does not have access to enough water. Many of these people live in Africa and Asia.

A bucket of water weighs about 10 kg (22 lbs.). Imagine if you had to carry a bucket or two from a well to your house every day.

North America has one-third the population of Africa, yet North Americans use three times as much water. How is this possible? Nearly 300 million people in Africa do not have access to enough freshwater.

Place — Average daily water use per person
1 bucket = 10 L (2.6 U.S. gal.)

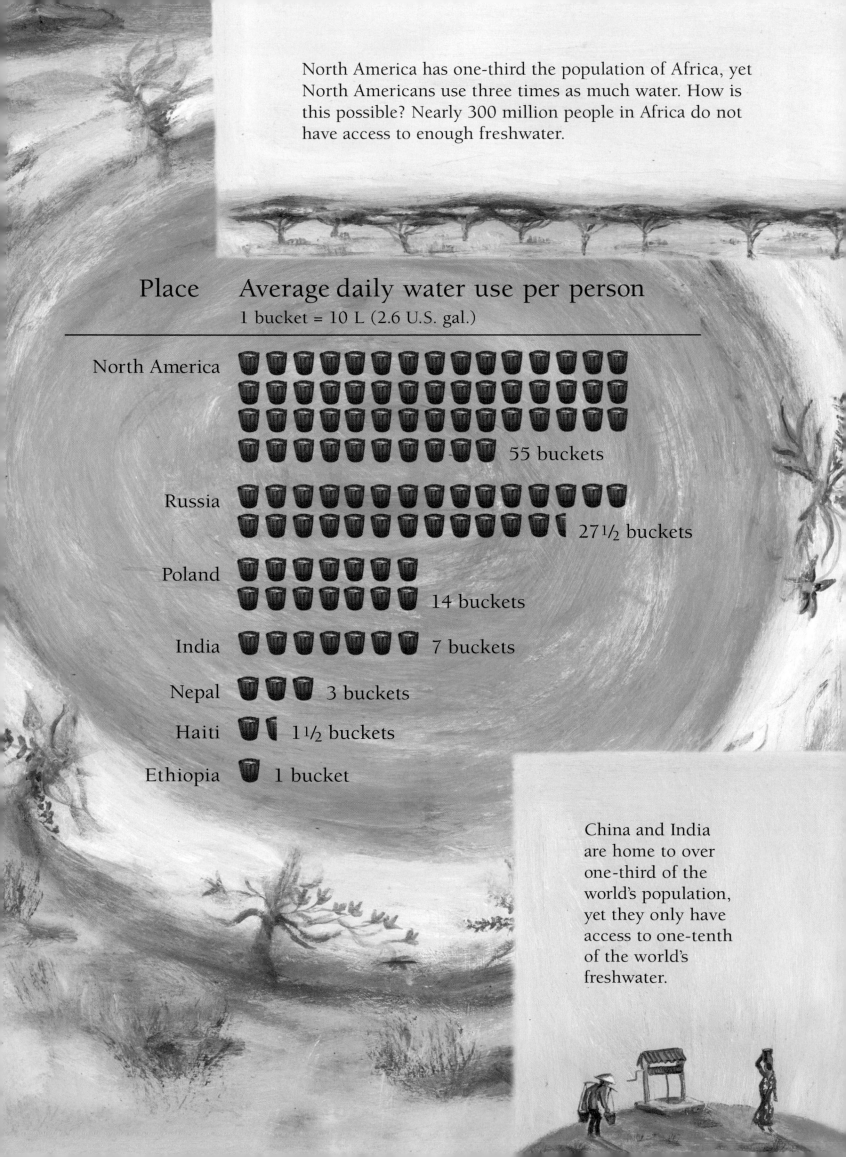

Place	Average daily water use per person
North America	55 buckets
Russia	27½ buckets
Poland	14 buckets
India	7 buckets
Nepal	3 buckets
Haiti	1½ buckets
Ethiopia	1 bucket

China and India are home to over one-third of the world's population, yet they only have access to one-tenth of the world's freshwater.

We need more and more water for crops and livestock in order to feed Earth's growing population.

By 2025, many experts predict that one out of every four people will live in a country that is short of water. By 2050, 4 billion people may be living without enough clean water.

Every day, all the world's livestock (cattle, sheep, pigs, goats, chickens) drink the equivalent of more than 160 000 large tanker trucks full of water.

Demands on the Well

7 021 836 029 … give or take a few. That's how many people there are on Earth, and that number is growing every day. More people mean a greater demand for water. But this growing population isn't the only thing putting a strain on our water supplies. The average person today uses about six times more water than a hundred years ago.

A growing population also means we need more space. As towns and cities grow to accommodate all these people, they gobble up land, which also affects nearby water. Houses, buildings and roads sometimes take the place of wetland habitats where animals live, which puts species at risk. They also change the way rainwater, lakes and streams flow. And pavement and concrete block rainwater from refilling underground water supplies.

There are more of us, and our demand for water at home, in industry and in agriculture has grown tremendously. But all the water we have is all the water we ever will have. There is no more water now than there was 100 or 1000 or even 10 000 years ago. And there will be no more 100 years from now, when the population may be closer to 10 billion.

We need to find a balance between our demands for water and the amount of water that's available to us.

While dams make more water available, they also change the flow of rivers and damage habitats.

Pollution in the Well

Water dissolves more things than any other liquid, so in nature, water is never really pure. It almost always has something dissolved in it.

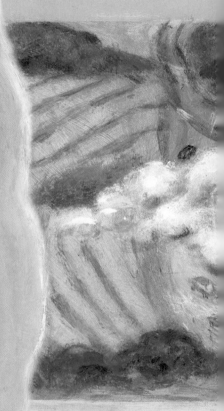

The water cycle helps keep Earth's water clean. As water evaporates, minerals, chemicals and dirt are left behind. The water vapor that rises into the atmosphere is relatively clean. When rain falls back to Earth, some of it is filtered through rocks and sand and is further cleaned. Even plants play a role. As water travels through them, plants remove chemicals in the water. Then they transpire clean water back into the air.

But more and more waste from industry, agriculture and homes is getting into the water. Runoff from backyards, city streets and farms dumps dirt and chemicals (such as pesticides, fertilizers and detergents) into lakes, rivers, streams and ponds. Pollution in the atmosphere from cars and factories mixes with water vapor in the air. The rain that falls pollutes surface water and groundwater. Our actions may be overloading water's natural ability to clean itself.

As more water becomes polluted, there is less clean water available. Nearly 80 percent of all sicknesses in the world are caused by unsafe water. And wildlife suffers, too. Water pollution threatens the health of many species and habitats across the planet.

Because of water's self-cleaning powers, the effects of pollution can be stopped and quite possibly reversed. But to do so, we need to reduce the amount of pollution that gets into the water.

Every day, 1.8 million tonnes (2 million tons) of garbage are dumped into Earth's water — enough to fill more than 15 000 boxcars.

Wetlands are nature's water treatment plants — they absorb chemicals and filter out pollution and waste.

When pollution in the air mixes with rain, it can turn into acid rain or even acid snow. This acid precipitation can fall thousands of kilometres (miles) from the source of the pollution, even reaching remote areas such as the Arctic.

Saving the Water in the Well

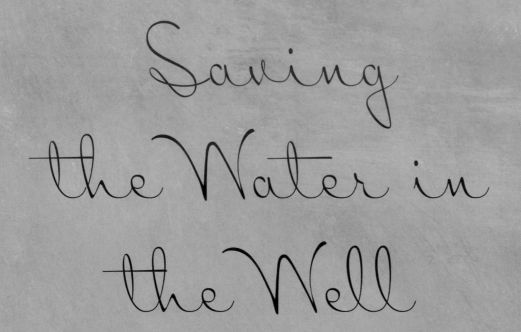

Water has the power to change everything. A single splash can sprout a seed, quench a thirst, provide a habitat, generate energy and sustain life. It also has the power to unite—or divide—the world. Water is the most basic and important need of all life on Earth.

But Earth's One Well is in trouble. There is simply not enough clean water to go around.

Taking actions to conserve water can help save the well. Conserving water means protecting both the quantity and quality of water on Earth. For example, using less water helps prevent water sources from drying up. And reducing water pollution protects the overall health of the well. Water conservation can help ensure there is enough clean water for everyone on the planet.

By becoming more aware of how you use water and by using less, you too can protect the water in Earth's One Well. Remember—every drop counts!

Becoming Well Aware

Water conservation isn't just something for governments, corporations and environmental groups to think about. Everyone needs to get involved in water conservation—even you. And it's not hard to do. It doesn't even mean living without water. It just means becoming "Well Aware" of every splash of water we use.

By reducing your water use, you too can become Well Aware. Even the simplest actions can make a huge difference. Imagine all the water you could save just by keeping drinking water in the fridge instead of letting the tap run to get cool water. And by making sure to turn off faucets so that they don't drip, you can save up to 10 000 L (2650 U.S. gal.) of water a year.

But becoming Well Aware doesn't just mean using less water, it also means taking better care of the water we have. You can protect water from pollution by walking more and driving less, which keeps car exhaust from polluting water in the atmosphere. Organizing shoreline cleanups keeps trash from entering lakes, rivers and streams. Planting trees anchors the soil so that it doesn't wash into waterways and make them muddy.

Imagine what would happen if each of us did just one thing to conserve water and protect Earth's One Well. These actions would add up. Together, they would help to ensure that there is enough clean water now and for years to come.

Here are just a few ways you can become Well Aware:

Learn More and Educate Others. By learning more about Earth's One Well, you can make choices in your life that help conserve and protect water. Then share what you learn. Help the people around you become Well Aware, too.

Join Others. There are many organizations working to protect water or helping people get the water they need. Find out more about organizations that interest you, and support their work by raising money, volunteering your time or helping to spread their message. Or start your own campaign.

Conserve Water. With your family, explore all the ways you use water and then brainstorm ways to reduce your water use at home. Some suggestions include:

- turning off the water while scrubbing your hands and brushing your teeth
- running the dishwasher and washing machine only when full
- asking your parents to fix leaky faucets
- collecting rainwater to water the plants in your garden or house
- watering your lawn only when it needs it and only in the early morning or evening, when less water will evaporate

Protect Water. Rainwater can wash waste and pollution into storm sewers, which flow into local rivers or lakes. Oil, grease, salt from roads, fertilizers and pesticides from gardens, paint, oil, leaves and litter can all end up in local waterways. Many communities paint fish or other symbols near sewers to remind people that sewers empty into waterways. Does your community have such a program? If not, why not try to start one.

Improving Access, One Well at a Time

More and more children and their families are becoming Well Aware. Some, like Ryan Hreljac, are helping to make water more accessible to those who need it most. In 1998, as a six year old, Ryan learned that many people in Africa didn't have access to clean water. He raised enough money to build a well near a school in Uganda. But he didn't stop there. With his parents' help, he started the Ryan's Well Foundation, which continues to raise money to build wells in Africa and educate people elsewhere about the need to conserve water.

NOTES TO PARENTS, GUARDIANS AND TEACHERS

A Crisis in the Well

Throughout human history, we have relied heavily on water. It has influenced nearly every aspect of our lives and livelihood. We've spent centuries learning how to harness water's incredible power and have become experts at catching and channeling it for our use. But our demand for water is growing rapidly and unsustainably. In our homes, we use six times more water now than we did a hundred years ago. Over the same period, the amount of irrigated land has more than doubled, greatly increasing water use. Industrial use has grown by almost four times since the 1950s alone.

And our growing consumption isn't the only problem. Other issues also threaten the health of Earth's One Well.

• Global warming and climate change affect weather and rainfall patterns around the world. As a result, some areas may experience extreme weather conditions and temperatures, which can lead to more flooding or drought. Over time, melting polar icecaps and warmer water may also cause sea levels to rise, altering the coastlines where many plants and animals live.

• Many of Earth's rivers cross international boundaries. But nations do not always work together to share this resource. Conflicts break out over who owns the water, how much is used and how it is used. How these fights are resolved will affect everyone.

• Habitats that surround the well are in crisis, too. Half of the world's wetlands have been drained. Dams have damaged habitats along 35 million km (22 million mi.) of the world's rivers. And some of the most threatened species on Earth are those that depend on watery habitats.

• Water treatment plants are not always effective at keeping harmful substances from entering the water cycle. They can barely handle all the water they currently process, so how will they handle more as demand grows? Treatment plants also use a tremendous amount of energy. An increasing demand for treated water poses a serious threat to the health of the well. And expanding, replacing or fixing water treatment plants will be very costly.

Helping Children Become Well Aware

As parents, teachers and guardians, we all have a role to play in helping our children understand the importance of water conservation. Only by fostering in them a sense of stewardship and responsibility for Earth's One Well can we teach our children to become Well Aware. Achieving this awareness will help children better understand the importance of all water on Earth and the issues facing the well. It will also foster a sense of compassion and understanding for the needs of people around the world, as well as other species and habitats.

Most important, by working with our

children to conserve and protect water — in our homes, schools, communities and in local habitats — we show them not just how to live sustainably within the water cycle, but also how their actions can make a difference. Encouraging, supporting and guiding our children to become Well Aware will give them the confidence to make decisions and take action, now and in the future, that will protect Earth's One Well.

What Can You Do?

• Get to know the issues. Learn more about the crisis facing Earth's One Well and make changes in your day-to-day activities to conserve water.

• Start a discussion with your children about the value of water. Have them imagine what would happen if there was no water when they turned on a tap. What would it be like to live without toilets, baths or showers? To walk ten minutes, thirty minutes or even an hour to get water? How would they use water differently? What things might they do without? Remind them that every day many people around the world don't have enough water to meet their needs.

• Celebrate the United Nation's International Decade for Action — Water for Life (2005 – 2015). The goal of this decade is to promote greater awareness of water-related issues. Work with your children to promote water awareness at home, at school, in your community, even in your city and country through water-oriented events, such as fairs, newsletters and invited speakers.

• Encourage your family or students to think critically about the water they use and the water they waste. Discuss and implement water conservation initiatives at home and at school. In your garden, try planting drought-tolerant and/or native species, collecting water in a rain barrel and recycling house water. You might also install water meters and water-saving plumbing, such as low-flush toilets. As you implement these and other water-saving initiatives, talk to your children about what you are doing and why.

• Adopt a waterway. With your family or as a class, select a local water body (river, lake, wetland, etc.) and research its history. How has the water been used over the years? How has your city or town developed around it? Has the flow of water changed (or been changed)? What issues currently threaten it? Prepare a newsletter on your findings and circulate it throughout your school and community. Remind readers that we all need to work together to protect these local water systems.

   We can no longer take it for granted that there will always be enough clean water for us, for our children or for our grandchildren. There is a crisis in the well and how we handle this crisis is one of the most important challenges facing the world today. Becoming Well Aware gives us all the power to protect Earth's One Well — and the potential to change the world.

INDEX